Quebec City Travel Guide 2023

Discover the Magic of Quebec City:

A Comprehensive Guide to the Culture, Cuisine, and Charm of this Historic Destination

Zak Thorpe

Quebec City Travel Guide 2023

All rights reserved. No part of this publication may be reproduced, distributed,or transmitted in any form or by any means, including photocopying, recording, or other electronic or mechanical methods, without the prior written permission of the publisher, except in the case of brief quotations embodied in critical reviews and certain other noncommercial uses permitted by copyright law.

Copyright © Zak Thorpe,2023.

Quebec City Travel Guide 2023

Table of contents

Introduction
- History of Quebec City

Chapter 1

Planning Your Trip
- Best Time to Visit Quebec City
- How to Get to Quebec City
- Where to Stay in Quebec City (Best Areas & Hotels)
- How to Get Around Quebec City
- Quebec City Passes and Discounts

Chapter 2

Exploring Quebec City
- Top Attractions in Quebec City

Quebec City Travel Guide 2023

- Museums and Art Galleries
- Parks and Gardens
- Historic Sites and Monuments
- Religious Sites and Buildings

Chapter 3

Food and Drink in Quebec City

- Quebec City Cuisines You Shouldn't Miss
- Best Restaurants in Quebec City
- Cafes and Bars

Chapter 4

Shopping in Quebec City

Chapter 5

Day Trips and Excursions from Quebec City

- Fun Things to Do in Quebec City

Chapter 6

Practical Information

Quebec City Travel Guide 2023

Chapter 7
Basic Phrases for Visitors in Quebec
Conclusion

Introduction

Quebec City is a spectacular setting that is rich in culture, history, and natural beauty. It is a city full of world-class attractions, such as world-class museums, art galleries, stunning architecture, scrumptious gastronomy, and a thriving entertainment scene.

The city is situated on the banks of the <u>St. Lawrence River</u>, and the scenic environment that surrounds it is just as beautiful as the city itself. The rolling hills, lush woodlands, and gleaming rivers serve as constant reminders of how crucial nature is to the character of Quebec City.

However, Quebec City's distinctiveness extends beyond the region's natural beauty. The city itself is an architectural and design marvel, with beautiful buildings and meandering cobblestone streets. It immediately transports you back in time. <u>The Historic Town</u> is particularly impressive, with its twisting alleys, small cafés, and spectacular ancient structures that have been lovingly preserved for decades.

One of Quebec City's most notable qualities is its vast history. <u>Samuel de Champlain</u> founded the city in 1608, and the city's numerous historic architecture and monuments bear witness to its long and famous past. <u>The Chateau Frontenac</u>, one of the city's most well-known attractions, allows tourists to walk about the historic Lower Town, examine the walls of the medieval defenses, and marvel at its stunning design.

Quebec City, on the other hand, is much more than a historical monument. This vibrant and dynamic city has a thriving arts and culture scene. Quebec City has a variety of attractions, including theaters, live music venues, and globally renowned museums and art galleries. The city is also widely recognized for its wonderful cuisine, which mixes indigenous, British, and French ingredients to create a truly unique eating experience.

Quebec City offers something for everyone, whether you're a history buff, an art lover, a gourmet, or just someone who likes traveling. The city is full of surprises, with secret passageways, tiny cafés, and unexpected panoramas around every corner.

However, the citizens of Quebec City are undoubtedly its most distinguishing attribute. Visitors to Quebec will get a warm welcome since the people of the province are known for their friendliness and kindness. The people of Quebec City are always willing to help, whether you're looking for restaurant recommendations, information on the top attractions, or just a pleasant discussion.

Finally, Quebec City is a spectacular site that will certainly attract your curiosity. Whether you're visiting for the first time or returning for a second visit, there's always something new to discover and enjoy. Why not pack your belongings, go to Quebec City, and experience the magic for yourself? You will not be disappointed!

History of Quebec City

Quebec City, situated in the province of Quebec, Canada, is one of the oldest cities in North America, with a long and rich history that has shaped its culture, architecture, and identity over the centuries. From its earliest days as a French colonial settlement to its role as a key player in the formation of modern Canada, Quebec City has played a central role in the history of the continent.

The First Inhabitants

Before the arrival of European settlers, the area now known as Quebec City was home to several Indigenous groups, including the Huron-Wendat, the Iroquois, and the Algonquin. These groups had been living in the region for thousands of years, fishing, hunting, and gathering resources from the land.

The Arrival of European Settlers

In 1535, French explorer Jacques Cartier arrived in the area and established a small settlement, which he named Stadacona, near what is now Quebec City. However, it was not until 1608 that permanent French settlement began in the area, when Samuel de Champlain, often referred to as the "*Father of New France*," founded the city of Quebec.

Champlain's goal was to establish a French presence in North America, which would allow for the expansion of the fur trade and the spread of Christianity. Quebec City was strategically located on the St. Lawrence River, which made it a key trading post and allowed for easy access to the interior of the continent.

Over the next century, the French colony in Quebec grew, with settlers establishing farms, trading posts, and missions throughout the region. However, relations with the Indigenous groups in the area were often fraught, with conflict over land, resources, and religion.

The British Conquest

In 1759, the British army, under the command of General James Wolfe, arrived in Quebec City, marking the beginning of a pivotal moment in the city's history. The French army, led by the Marquis de Montcalm, fought back fiercely, but in the end, the British emerged victorious. <u>The Battle of the Plains of Abraham,</u> fought just outside the city walls, is considered one of the most significant battles in Canadian history.

Following the conquest, the British took control of Quebec City and established a new government, which would remain in place until the formation of modern Canada in 1867. Despite the change in political control, the French language, culture, and traditions continued to thrive in Quebec City, and the city remained an important center of commerce, culture, and politics.

The Quiet Revolution

In the 1960s, Quebec experienced a period of social, political, and cultural upheaval, known as the Quiet Revolution. During this time, Quebecers began to assert their distinct identity and demand greater autonomy from the rest of Canada.

The Quiet Revolution had a profound impact on Quebec City, with the city becoming a center of cultural and political activism. The city's architecture and design also underwent a significant transformation, with modernist buildings and infrastructure replacing older, traditional structures.

Modern-Day Quebec City
Today, Quebec City is a vibrant and dynamic city, home to a diverse population of over 844,000 people. It is a key center of French culture and language in North America, and is renowned for its stunning architecture, rich history, and thriving arts and culture scene.

Visitors to Quebec City can explore the city's many historic sites and monuments, including the ramparts of the old fortifications, the historic Lower Town, and the stunning architecture of the Chateau Frontenac. The city is also home to world-class museums and art galleries, as well as a lively entertainment scene, with live music venues, theaters, and festivals throughout the year.

In recent years, Quebec City has also emerged as a hub for technology, innovation, and entrepreneurship, with a growing startup scene and a range of high-tech industries, including gaming, software development, and biotechnology.

Despite its modernization and growth, Quebec City has managed to preserve its rich history and cultural heritage. The city's architecture, with its distinctive blend of French and British styles, has been carefully maintained and restored, and many of the city's historic buildings and landmarks have been designated as UNESCO World Heritage sites.

Quebec City is also known for its vibrant and unique culture, which draws on its rich history and diverse population. The city's cuisine, for example, is a fusion of French, Indigenous, and other international influences, and is celebrated for its use of fresh, local ingredients and bold flavors. Quebec City is also famous for its music, literature, and arts scene, which has produced some of Canada's most influential and celebrated artists.

In recent years, Quebec City has also become known for its commitment to sustainability and environmental stewardship. The city has implemented a range of initiatives aimed at reducing its carbon footprint and promoting sustainable development, including a network of bike paths and a public transportation system that runs on renewable energy.

Overall, the history of Quebec City is a complex and fascinating story, spanning thousands of years and encompassing a wide range of cultures, peoples, and events. From its origins as an Indigenous settlement to its role as a key player in the formation of modern Canada, Quebec City has played an important role in shaping the history and culture of the continent. Today, it continues to be a vibrant and dynamic city, celebrated for its rich history, stunning architecture, and unique cultural identity.

Chapter 1

Planning Your Trip

Planning a trip can be both exciting and overwhelming. There are so many details to consider, from choosing a destination to booking accommodations, transportation, and activities. If you're planning a trip to Quebec City in 2023, here are some tips to help you plan a memorable and stress-free trip.

Best Time to Visit Quebec City

Quebec City is a vibrant destination that can be enjoyed year-round, with each season offering its own unique charm and activities. The best time to visit will depend on your interests and preferences, as well as your budget and availability.

1. **Summer (June to August)**

Summer is the most popular time to visit Quebec City, with warm temperatures and a lively atmosphere. The city comes alive with festivals, outdoor concerts, and street performers. The most famous event of the summer is the Quebec City Summer Festival, which brings in renowned musical acts from all over the world. The Old Town and the surrounding parks and gardens are at their best during this season, with colorful flowers and trees in full bloom. However, summer is also the busiest time of the year, with crowds and higher prices.

2. **Fall (September to November)**

Fall is a beautiful time to visit Quebec City, with crisp temperatures and stunning autumn foliage. The city is less crowded than in the summer, making it a great time to explore the historic Old Town and the nearby parks and forests. The Festival of New France takes place in August and September, celebrating Quebec's colonial history with reenactments, music, and food. The city also hosts a variety of fall festivals, including the International Literary Festival and the Quebec City Film Festival.

3. Winter (December to February)

Winter is a magical time to visit Quebec City, with snow-covered streets and a festive atmosphere. The city hosts one of the most famous winter festivals in the world, the Quebec Winter Carnival, which takes place in February. The festival features ice sculptures, parades, concerts, and winter sports. The Old Town is especially enchanting during this season, with its charming Christmas markets and ice-skating rinks. However, winter can be quite cold, with temperatures often dropping below freezing.

4. **Spring (March to May)**

Spring is a beautiful time to visit Quebec City, with milder temperatures and fewer crowds. The city comes to life with the arrival of spring, with blooming flowers and trees and outdoor activities such as hiking and cycling. The Quebec City International Auto Show takes place in April, showcasing the latest in automotive technology. The city also hosts a variety of spring festivals, including the Quebec City International Festival of Animated Films and the Quebec City International Sacred Music Festival.

In conclusion, Quebec City is a destination that can be enjoyed year-round, with each season offering its own unique activities and charm. Whether you prefer warm summer days, colorful fall foliage, festive winter celebrations, or blooming spring flowers, Quebec City has something to offer for everyone.

How to Get to Quebec City

Getting to Quebec City is easy, with several options available to suit your budget and preferences. Whether you prefer to travel by air, train, car, or bus, there are plenty of options to choose from.

1. By Air

The Jean Lesage International Airport (YQB) is located just 20 minutes from downtown Quebec City, making it the most convenient option for visitors arriving from out of town. The airport is served by several major airlines, including Air Canada, WestJet, Delta, and United. Non-stop flights are available from several North American cities, including New York, Toronto, Montreal, Chicago, and Boston. From the airport, you can take a taxi, shuttle, or public transit to your accommodations. Car rental companies are also available at the airport.

2. By Train

If you prefer to travel by train, Via Rail operates several daily trains to Quebec City from Montreal and Toronto. The trains offer scenic views of the countryside and are a comfortable and convenient way to travel. The train station is located just outside of the Old Town, and taxis and public transit are available to take you to your accommodations.

3. By Car
If you prefer to drive, Quebec City is easily accessible by car, with several highways leading to the city. From Montreal, you can take Highway 40, which takes approximately 2.5 hours. From Toronto, you can take Highway 401 to Highway 20, which takes approximately 8.5 hours. Parking in the Old Town can be challenging, so it is recommended to park in one of the nearby parking lots and walk to your accommodations.

4. By Bus
Several bus companies operate daily services to Quebec City from Montreal, Ottawa, and Toronto, including Greyhound and Orléans Express. The bus station is located just outside of the Old

Town, and taxis and public transit are available to take you to your accommodations.

Once you arrive in Quebec City, the city is relatively easy to navigate on foot, with the Old Town being the main attraction. Public transit is also available, with buses and a metro system connecting the city's neighborhoods. Taxis and ride-sharing services are also available for those who prefer a more private mode of transportation.

In conclusion, getting to Quebec City is easy and convenient, with several options available to suit your budget and preferences. Whether you prefer to travel by air, train, car, or bus, you can easily reach this vibrant destination and start exploring all that it has to offer.

Where to Stay in Quebec City (Best Areas & Hotels)

When planning a trip to Quebec City, choosing the right area to stay is essential to make the most of your visit. Whether you are looking for historic charm, luxury accommodations, or a vibrant nightlife, there is a neighborhood in Quebec City that will fit your preferences. Below, we will explore the best areas to stay in Quebec City and recommend some of the best hotels to make your trip unforgettable.

1. Old Quebec (Vieux-Québec)

Old Quebec is the historic heart of the city and is a UNESCO World Heritage site. It is a charming neighborhood with cobblestone streets, charming boutiques, and beautiful architecture that will transport you back in time. Staying in Old

Quebec will put you in the heart of the action, with many of the city's main attractions within walking distance, including the Château Frontenac, the Citadelle, and the Place Royale. There are plenty of hotels to choose from in Old Quebec, ranging from boutique hotels to luxury accommodations. Some of the best hotels in Old Quebec include the Fairmont Le Château Frontenac, Auberge Saint-Antoine, and Hotel 71.

2. Saint-Roch

If you are looking for a more contemporary vibe, Saint-Roch is the place to be. This trendy neighborhood is home to some of the city's best restaurants, bars, and boutiques. Staying in Saint-Roch will put you close to the city's emerging arts scene, including the Musée de la Civilisation and the Grand Théâtre de Québec. Some of the best hotels in Saint-Roch include the <u>Hotel PUR Quebec</u>, <u>Auberge Saint-Louis</u>, and <u>Hotel des Coutellier</u>.

3. **Montcalm**

Montcalm is a picturesque neighborhood located just outside of Old Quebec. It is a residential area with beautiful tree-lined streets and grand mansions, making it a great choice for those looking for a more peaceful stay. Staying in Montcalm will put you within walking distance of the Plains of Abraham and the Musée National des Beaux-Arts du Québec. Some of the best hotels in Montcalm include the <u>Hotel Château Laurier,</u> <u>Le Grande-Allée Hotel & Suites,</u> and <u>Hotel Manoir Victoria</u>.

4. **Lower Town (Basse-Ville)**

Lower Town is located at the bottom of the hill below Old Quebec and is home to some of the city's oldest buildings. This neighborhood is a great choice for those looking to stay in a more affordable area without sacrificing location. Staying in Lower Town will put you within walking distance of the _Quartier Petit Champlain,_ the oldest commercial district in North America. Some of the best hotels in Lower Town include the _Hotel du Vieux-Québec, Hotel Sainte-Anne,_ and _Hotel Le Saint-Paul._

5. **Saint-Jean-Baptiste**

Saint-Jean-Baptiste is a trendy neighborhood located just outside of Old Quebec. It is home to some of the city's best restaurants and bars, as well as the famous _Cartier Avenue_. Staying in Saint-Jean-Baptiste will put you within walking distance of the city's vibrant nightlife scene. Some of the best hotels in Saint-Jean-Baptiste include the _Hotel Le_

Germain Quebec, Hotel Hippocampe, and Le 760.

In conclusion, choosing the right area to stay in Quebec City is essential to make the most of your visit. Whether you are looking for historic charm, luxury accommodations, or a vibrant nightlife, there is a neighborhood in Quebec City that will fit your preferences. From the charming cobblestone streets of Old Quebec to the trendy vibe of Saint-Roch, there is something for everyone in Quebec City.

How to Get Around Quebec City

Getting around Quebec City is easy and convenient, whether you prefer walking, public transportation, or driving. The city is relatively compact, and many of the main attractions are within walking distance of each other. Below, we will explore the different transportation options available in Quebec City to help you get around with ease.

1. Walking

Walking is one of the best ways to explore Quebec City. The city's compact size and pedestrian-friendly streets make it easy to get around on foot. You can wander through the charming cobblestone streets of Old Quebec, take a stroll along the Saint Lawrence River, or explore the parks and gardens of the city. Walking is also a great way to discover hidden gems and take in the city's beautiful architecture.

2. Public Transportation

Quebec City has an efficient public transportation system, including buses and trains, that can take you to all parts of the city. The Réseau de Transport de la

Capitale (RTC) operates a network of buses that run throughout the city and surrounding areas. The buses are clean, safe, and reliable, and the fares are affordable. You can purchase tickets on board the bus, at vending machines, or at designated ticket outlets.

The Société de transport de Lévis (STLévis) operates a ferry service that connects Quebec City to the city of Lévis on the other side of the Saint Lawrence River. The ferry offers stunning views of the city and is a great way to experience the river. The ferry runs throughout the day and evening and it is affordable.

3. Taxis and Ridesharing

Taxis and ridesharing services such as Uber are available in Quebec City. Taxis are readily available throughout the city, and you can flag one down on the street or call a taxi company to book a ride. Ridesharing services such as Uber are also available in Quebec City, and you can use the app to request a ride.

4. **Biking**

Biking is a popular mode of transportation in Quebec City, especially during the warmer months. The city has an extensive network of bike paths and lanes that make it easy to get around on two wheels. You can rent a bike from one of the many bike rental shops in the city, including those located in Old Quebec.

5. **Driving**

If you prefer to drive, Quebec City has a well-developed road network that connects the city to other parts of the region. However, driving in the city can be challenging, especially in Old Quebec, where the streets are narrow and parking can be limited. If you plan to drive in the city, it is recommended to use a GPS navigation system or a map to help you navigate.

Quebec City Passes and Discounts

Quebec City is a beautiful and historic city that has a lot to offer visitors. From the charming cobblestone streets of Old Quebec to the stunning views of the Saint Lawrence River, there are countless attractions and activities to enjoy in this city. However, the cost of visiting all of these attractions can add up quickly, especially if you are traveling on a budget. Fortunately, there are several Quebec City passes and discounts available that can help you save money on your trip. Below, we will explore some of the best Quebec City passes and discounts that can help

Quebec City Travel Guide 2023

you make the most of your trip without breaking the bank.

1. Quebec City Museum Pass

If you are interested in art, history, and culture, the Quebec City Museum Pass is an excellent choice. This pass gives you access to 11 museums and art galleries in Quebec City, including the *Museum of Civilization*, the *Quebec National Museum of Fine Arts*, and the *Museum of French America*. With this pass, you can explore the city's rich history and culture at your own pace, and save money at the same time. The pass is valid for three consecutive days and costs $68 CAD for adults.

2. Quebec City Attractions Pass

The Quebec City Attractions Pass is another excellent choice for visitors who want to see the best of what the city has to offer. This pass gives you access to several popular attractions in Quebec City, including the Quebec City Observatory, the Musée de la Civilisation, and the Aquarium du Québec. The pass also includes discounts on other activities and tours in the city. The pass is valid for either 1, 2, or 3 consecutive days, and prices start at $54 CAD.

3. Old Quebec Walking Tour Pass

If you want to explore the charming cobblestone streets and historic buildings of Old Quebec, the Old Quebec Walking Tour Pass is a great option. This pass gives you access to three different walking tours of Old Quebec, including the Upper Town Tour, the Lower Town Tour, and the Ghosts and Legends Tour. The tours are led by experienced guides who will share the history and stories of the city as you explore its streets. The pass is valid for 24 hours and costs $25 CAD.

4. Public Transportation Pass

If you plan to use public transportation to get around Quebec City, the RTC Pass is an excellent choice. This pass gives you unlimited access to the city's bus and train network for a specified period, from 1 to 30 days. The pass is an affordable option for visitors who plan to use public transportation frequently during their stay in Quebec City. Prices vary depending on the duration of the pass, but a 3-day pass costs $23 CAD.

5. Student Discounts

If you are a student, there are several Quebec City passes and discounts available that can help you save money on your trip. Many of the city's museums and attractions offer discounted admission for students, and the RTC Pass also offers a discount for students with a valid student ID. Additionally, the Quebec City Student Card is a great option for students who want to save money on dining, entertainment, and shopping in the city. The card costs $19.99 CAD and is valid for one year.

In conclusion, Quebec City passes and discounts can help you save money on your trip and make the most of your time in this beautiful city. Whether you want to explore the city's museums and galleries, its historic streets, or its public transportation network, there is a pass or discount available that will suit your needs. By taking advantage of these options, you can enjoy all that Quebec City has to offer without breaking the bank.

Chapter 2

Exploring Quebec City

Top Attractions in Quebec City

Here are a few must-see places in Quebec City that you should not miss as you plan your vacation to the city and learn about its rich history, culture, language, and surroundings.

1. The Old Port Market

Stroll over to this covered market, which has a range of food sellers, for a sample of regional cuisine and innovative culinary treats. From a selection of fresh fruit and vegetable choices, deli items, maple syrup, ice wine, and more, you may choose the perfect souvenir or build a picnic lunch to enjoy anywhere in the Old Port.

2. The Capital Watchtower

On the 31st floor of the Marie-Guyart Building, the Observatoire de la Capitale provides the best panoramic view of Quebec City. The observatory has a wall-to-wall visual narrative of Quebec City's history and provides stunning year-round panoramic views from the city's tallest structure.

3. Montmorency Falls

The Chute Montmorency, also known as Montmorency Falls, is 30 meters (98 feet) higher than Niagara Falls, which stands 83 meters (272 feet). The magnificent waterfall is accessible by driving from downtown Quebec City (or by bike during the warmer months), and it is a popular year-round activity.

4. Seasonal festivities

Aside from the well-known *Carnaval de Québec* and the *Festival d'été de Québec,* you should also attend *Le Festival ComediHa!* in June, where at least one English comedian performs every night, and *Le Festibière de Québec,* a beer festival where you can sample local ciders, wines, produce, and other samples in an outdoor setting, as well as the distinct flavors created by Quebec's microbreweries and brewpubs.

5. Toboggan Slide Au 1884

The Toboggan Slide Au 1884 is a popular winter pastime for both locals and tourists. This massive snow slide, one of Quebec City's oldest attractions, starts at the Terrasse Dufferin and runs into the city center. Riding a classic wooden toboggan that can carry up to four riders, you may achieve speeds of up to 70kph (43mph).

6. **The Plains of Abraham**

The Plains of Abraham, which is now a recreational public park, is one of Canada's most important historical sites. In 1759, British soldiers beat French forces in a fight that would eventually play an important part in the formation of North American history. Depending on the season, consider enjoying a picnic or partaking in some cycling, cross-country skiing, or other sports on the plateau.

7. **La Citadelle**

In Quebec City, a star-shaped citadel known as La Citadelle was built atop *Cap Diamant*. It was created in the 1800s to safeguard the city from an impending American invasion, and it today serves as the command headquarters for the Royal 22nd Regiment of Canada.

8. The Ice Hotel

The magnificent _Hôtel de Glace_ is a unique wintertime resort near Quebec City's core. You may visit this masterpiece composed of tons of ice and snow for a day trip or stay overnight if you brave the bitter cold.

9. The Frontenac Inn

This antique hotel seems to be from a fairy tale. Spend the night at this hotel, which is famed for being the most photographed in the world, or take a tour during the day to discover more about one of Quebec City's most well-known sites.

10. The Fine Arts Department of the National Museum of Quebec

The Musée National des Beaux-arts du Québec, one of the city's main international museums, contains three pavilions featuring 25,000 pieces made in Quebec or by Quebecois painters, many of which date back to the 18th century, as well as more than 2,500 examples of Inuit art.

11. Civilizations Assortment

The Musée de la Civilisation is one of Canada's most popular museums, with over 14 million visitors each year. Explore the many current and passing exhibits, multimedia displays, and interactive stations that provide insights into the history of Quebec, Aboriginal peoples, and other regions of the globe.

12. The Fortifications

The only walled city north of Mexico that has remained is situated in Old Quebec and is a Unesco World Heritage Site. The fortifications that encircle Quebec City have weathered three centuries of vigorous colonial history. The fortifications also provide breathtaking views of the city below.

13. Quarter of Petit Champlain

Quartier Petit Champlain was one of North America's original commercial districts. Along the cobblestone lanes of the neighborhood, which is part of Vieux-Québec, are a variety of art galleries, cafés, and souvenir stores. The Breakneck Stairs, Quebec City's oldest stairway, were completed in 1635 and should not be missed.

14. Quebec Aquarium

The Aquarium du Québec is home to about 10,000 animals, including fish, amphibians, reptiles, invertebrates, and marine mammals. Thousands of tourists visit the aquarium each year, which is a one-of-a-kind attraction in the province and is just 15 minutes from downtown Quebec City.

15. The Ursuline Museum

The art and history museum known as the Musée des Ursulines de Québec provides an essential view into the women who moved from Europe to New France during the province's early formation. This little, attractive museum has almost 30,000 artifacts and provides tourists with a calm retreat in the heart of Old Quebec.

16. Battlefields Park

Battlefields Park, with a total area of 103 hectares (254.5 acres), comprises the

Plains of Abraham and a variety of monuments, structures, and displays connected to Canada's early military history. Visit the interpretive center on-site for more information on the park's and the surrounding area's history.

17. The Trésor Path

The Rue du Trésor is a delightful outdoor gallery set in a small Quebec City alley that transports you to medieval Europe. It was founded by art students in the 1960s and is still a flourishing cultural hub today.

18. Terrasse Dufferin

Terrasse Dufferin, an open park created in 1879 that stretches from the Chateau Frontenac to La Citadelle, has a wooden promenade with gazebos and seating. In the summer, it is a popular spot for strolling, relaxing, and people-watching, and from December to March, it hosts the annual toboggan run.

19. Notre-Dame Basilica-Cathedral in Quebec

The Basilique Cathedrale - Notre-Dame-de-Québec, which was established on the site in 1647, has been damaged by fire multiple times over its history. Numerous prominent personalities from New France's theological and political history are buried in the cathedral's crypt, which is a National Historic Site of Canada. Come for the interior's stunning artwork and architecture.

20. Place Royale

The Place Royale in Old Quebec is a notable historical monument in Canada. The neighborhood, which was built in the 17th century with a combination of buildings and streets, is today home to a variety of boutiques, diners, cafés, and stores. The Notre-Dame-des-Victoires church is one of the oldest stone churches in North America and should not be missed.

Museums and Art Galleries

Quebec City is a city that is rich in culture and history, and as such, it is home to a variety of museums and art galleries that offer visitors a glimpse into its past and present. Whether you are interested in art, history, or science, there is something for everyone in Quebec City's museums and art galleries.

One of the most popular museums in Quebec City is the **_Musée de la Civilisation._** This museum is dedicated to the history and culture of Quebec and features exhibits on everything from the history of the province to its contemporary culture. The museum is also home to a children's museum and a range of interactive exhibits that make it a fun and engaging experience for visitors of all ages.

For art lovers, the **_Musée National des Beaux-Arts du Québec_** is a must-visit attraction. This beautiful museum is home to a wide range of artwork, from contemporary pieces to historic masterpieces. The museum is also home to a beautiful sculpture garden, which is a perfect place to relax and enjoy the beauty of the art.

Another popular museum in Quebec City is the **_Musée de la Place Royale_**, which is dedicated to the history of Quebec City's oldest neighborhood. The museum features exhibits on everything from the city's early days as a French colony to its modern history as a bustling metropolis.

For those interested in science, the **Quebec Aquarium** is a must-visit attraction. This aquarium is home to a wide range of marine life, including sharks, sea turtles, and beluga whales. Visitors can also take part in a variety of interactive exhibits and shows that explore the science and conservation of the marine world.

If you are interested in history, the **Citadelle of Quebec** is a must-see attraction. This historic fort was built in the 19th century and is home to a museum that explores the military history of Quebec City and Canada. Visitors can also take a guided tour of the fort and learn about its history and architecture.

For those interested in contemporary art, the **Galerie d'Art du Chateau Frontenac** is a must-visit attraction. This beautiful gallery is located in the iconic Château Frontenac and features a wide range of contemporary art from both local and international artists.

Overall, Quebec City's museums and art galleries offer visitors a unique glimpse into the city's culture, history, and artistic heritage. Whether you are a history buff, an art lover, or simply curious about the world around you, there is something for everyone in Quebec City's museums and art galleries.

Parks and Gardens

Quebec City is not only rich in culture and history, but it is also home to a wide range of parks and gardens that offer visitors a chance to relax and enjoy the beauty of nature. From beautifully manicured gardens to sprawling parks with stunning views, there is something for everyone in Quebec City's parks and gardens.

One of the most popular parks in Quebec City is the **Plains of Abraham**. This beautiful park is located in the heart of the city and is home to over 100 hectares of open green space, walking trails, and picnic areas. The park is also home to the **Joan of Arc Garden,** a beautiful garden that features a variety of flowers and plants that bloom throughout the year.

Another popular park in Quebec City is the **Bois-de-Coulonge Park**. This beautiful park is located just outside the city center and is home to over 90 hectares of forested land, walking trails, and gardens. The park is also home to the historic _Maison Henry-Stuart,_ a beautiful 19th-century mansion that is open to the public for tours.

For those interested in botanical gardens, the **_Jardin Botanique Roger-Van den Hende_** is a must-visit attraction. This beautiful garden is located just outside the city center and is home to a wide range of plants and flowers from around the world. Visitors can take a guided tour of the garden and learn about its history and the different plants that call it home.

Another popular park in Quebec City is the **_Parc de la Chute-Montmorency_**. This beautiful park is located just outside the city and is home to the stunning Montmorency Falls, which is over 80 meters tall. Visitors can take a cable car to the top of the falls or explore the park's walking trails that offer stunning views of the falls and the surrounding area.

For those interested in history, the **Battlefields Park** is a must-visit attraction. This historic park is home to a variety of monuments and memorials that commemorate the battles that took place on the Plains of Abraham during the Seven Years' War and the Battle of Sainte-Foy. Visitors can also explore the park's walking trails and enjoy the stunning views of the city and the St. Lawrence River.

Overall, Quebec City's parks and gardens offer visitors a chance to escape the hustle and bustle of the city and enjoy the beauty of nature. Whether you are interested in botanical gardens, historic parks, or simply a place to relax and enjoy the sunshine, there is something for everyone in Quebec City's parks and gardens.

Historic Sites and Monuments

1. Chateau Frontenac

One of the most iconic landmarks in Quebec City, the Chateau Frontenac is a grand hotel that dates back to 1893. It sits atop a hill overlooking the St. Lawrence River and is a must-see attraction for visitors to the city.

2. Citadel of Quebec

Located on a hill overlooking the city, the Citadel of Quebec is a star-shaped fortification that was built in the early 19th century. It is still an active military installation and visitors can take guided tours of the site.

Quebec City Travel Guide 2023

3. Notre-Dame de Quebec Basilica-Cathedral

This historic cathedral is located in the heart of the Old City and dates back to the 17th century. It is a beautiful example of French-Canadian religious architecture and is open to the public for tours.

4. Place Royale

Known as the birthplace of French America, Place Royale is a historic square that dates back to the 17th century. It is home to a variety of historic buildings and is a popular spot for visitors to take photos and explore the city's history.

5. Fortifications of Quebec

The fortifications of Quebec are a UNESCO World Heritage Site and include a variety of walls, gates, and other defensive structures that were built to protect the city. Visitors can take guided

Copyrighted material © 57

tours of the fortifications and learn about their history.

6. Morrin Centre

Originally built as a jail in the 19th century, the Morrin Centre is now a cultural center that includes a library, museum, and historic building. Visitors can take guided tours of the site and learn about its history and role in Quebec City's cultural heritage.

7. Martello Towers

Quebec City is home to four Martello Towers, which were built in the 19th century to defend the city against potential American attacks. Visitors can take guided tours of the towers and learn about their history and importance to the city's defense.

8. Parliament Building

Quebec City is the capital of the province of Quebec, and the Parliament Building is the seat of government. The building is open to the public for guided tours, and visitors can learn about the history of the province and its government.

9. **Montmorency Falls**

Although not technically a historic site or monument, Montmorency Falls is a natural wonder that is worth visiting. It is located just outside the city and is over 80 meters tall. Visitors can take a cable car to the top of the falls or explore the walking trails that offer stunning views of the falls and the surrounding area.

10. **Artillery Park**

Located in the heart of the city, Artillery Park is a historic site that includes a variety of buildings and structures that date back to the 18th century. Visitors can take guided tours of the site and learn about its history and importance to the city's defense.

Religious Sites and Buildings

1. Notre-Dame de Quebec Basilica-Cathedral

This beautiful cathedral is a must-see attraction in Quebec City. It is the oldest church in Canada and is one of the few remaining examples of French religious architecture in North America. The cathedral features stunning stained glass windows, intricate wood carvings, and impressive works of art.

2. Sainte-Anne-de-Beaupré Shrine

Located just outside Quebec City, the Sainte-Anne-de-Beaupré Shrine is a major pilgrimage site for Catholics. The shrine is dedicated to Saint Anne, the mother of the Virgin Mary, and features a basilica, a museum, and a variety of other religious buildings and structures. Visitors can attend Mass or explore the site's many exhibits and displays.

3. **Ursulines Monastery**

The Ursulines Monastery is a historic convent that dates back to the 17th century. It is the oldest institution of learning for women in North America and is still home to a community of Ursuline nuns. Visitors can take guided tours of the monastery and learn about its history and role in the development of Quebec City.

4. **Saint-Jean-Baptiste Church**

This historic church is located in the heart of the Saint-Jean-Baptiste neighborhood and is a beautiful example of neo-Gothic architecture. The church features stunning stained glass windows and intricate wood carvings, and is still an active parish in Quebec City.

5. Eglise Saint-Roch

Located in the Saint-Roch neighborhood, Eglise Saint-Roch is a historic church that dates back to the mid-19th century. It features stunning stained glass windows and beautiful works of art, and is a popular destination for visitors to Quebec City.

6. Jesuit Chapel of the Holy Family

This small chapel is located in the heart of the Old City and is a hidden gem that is often overlooked by visitors. The chapel dates back to the mid-18th century and features beautiful Baroque architecture and stunning works of art.

7. Monastère des Augustines

The Monastère des Augustines is a historic convent that was founded by the Augustinian Sisters in the 17th century. Today, the site has been transformed into a wellness center and museum, where visitors can learn about the history of the convent and explore its many exhibits and displays.

8. Chapelle des Ursulines

This small chapel is located in the heart of the Old City and is a beautiful example of French religious architecture. The chapel features stunning stained glass windows and intricate wood carvings, and is a popular destination for visitors to Quebec City.

9. Chapelle Notre-Dame-de-Lourdes

Located in the Saint-Sauveur neighborhood, the Chapelle Notre-Dame-de-Lourdes is a historic church that dates back to the early 20th century. It features beautiful stained glass windows and impressive works of art, and is still an active parish in Quebec City.

10. Basilique-cathédrale Notre-Dame-de-l'Assomption Located in the nearby city of Trois-Rivières, the Basilique-cathédrale Notre-Dame-de-l'Assomption is a stunning example of religious architecture. The basilica features beautiful stained glass windows and impressive works of art, and is a popular destination for visitors to Quebec City.

Chapter 3

Food and Drink in Quebec City

The food and drink scene in Quebec City is rich in history and culture, influenced by the city's French, British, and Indigenous heritage. The city's culinary identity is rooted in farm-to-table cuisine, traditional Quebecois dishes, and an abundance of local ingredients.

Quebec City has a long history of food and drink, dating back to the 1600s when French settlers first arrived in the area. The French brought with them their culinary traditions, and over time these blended with the Indigenous food culture. Today, the city's cuisine is an amalgamation of these influences, with modern twists and techniques.

Quebec City Cuisines You Shouldn't Miss

1. Poutine (French fries with cheese curds)

Poutine is a delectable delicacy that comprises finely cut potato chips coated with semi-creamy cheese curds and sauce. Some locals would advise against it since it has so many calories and is terrible for weight maintenance. It means "_mess_" in Quebecois slang! It's neither visually beautiful nor healthy, but it's delicious.

Despite its popularity throughout Canada, the meal is said to have originated in Quebec. Poutine may be found everywhere in Quebec City, from sophisticated luxury restaurants to franchise locations and tucked-away cafes. Toppings such as jerked pork, streaky bacon, and smoked beef are among the inventive varieties.

2. **Soupe aux pois (pea soup)**

Soupe aux pois, a substantial and nourishing pea soup meal, originated during the colonial period. Samuel de Champlain's ships were stocked with dried beans and salted pork when he arrived in New France over 400 years ago. Chefs prepared a nourishing soup known as "_habitant pea soup_" in commemoration of the first Quebec settlers to feed the settlers.

The meal eventually changed as new foods were accessible. The bulk of contemporary variations features a bay leaf-seasoned soup with vegetables, salted pork, and yellow peas. It's also a classic sugar shack meal that's usually served as the main course.

3. **Viande fumée (smoked Montreal beef)**

Even though this Quebec delicacy originated in Montreal, it is also widely eaten there. Reuben Schwartz, a Romanian immigrant, invented this pastrami-like smoked beef in 1928, and it rapidly became famous among the area's gourmets. The dish was popular in Jewish delicatessens of the time because it was completely kosher.

For around ten days, a beef brisket known as viande fumée is marinated with herbs and spices. After being cured and smoked, the soft, meaty delight is chopped into thick rye bread sandwiches. Pickles, coleslaw, peppers, mustard, and olives round out the bundle.

4. **French-Canadian crêpes**

French-Canadian crêpes are fluffy, pancake-like dishes that may be filled with either sweet or savory ingredients. There is a distinction between French and French-Canadian crêpes made using buckwheat flour. The local version is a little thicker and has somewhat crisper edges than the European version. However, if you've tasted French crêpes before, you'll probably know what to anticipate.

Crêpes have a high level of adaptability. Sweet crêpes topped with strawberries, bananas, and whipped cream make a delicious dessert. If you prefer, a full breakfast with ham, cheese, a poached egg, and Hollandaise sauce is available. A crepe may satisfy all of your cravings.

5. **Tourtière, (Quebecois meat pie)**

Pork pies produced in the Quebecois style known as tourtière are popular during the holidays. The flaky, pastry-wrapped delicacy, packed with spicy pig or cow mince, is a long-standing end-of-year tradition in Quebec. The dish is called pâté à la viande in various parts of the province.

Some cooks combine spices like cinnamon, nutmeg, and cloves with vegetables like chopped potatoes and onions. Despite regional and familial differences, the meal is virtually always eaten around brunch or breakfast towards the end of the year. Tourtière is a traditional Christmas tradition in many Quebecois homes.

6. **Fèves au lard, (baked beans)**

Fèves au lard are baked beans that have been seasoned with fat and sweetened with maple syrup. The calorie-dense lunch was originally intended to give early lumberjacks and hunters adequate energy for a full day of effort. From office professionals to hungover students, the lavish morning brunch has become a favorite among all sorts of Quebecers.

Au lard is a French phrase that translates to "*fatty*" in English and refers to the salted ham or swine hocks used to steep slow-cooked beans. In the custom of Quebec, the dish is heavily topped with locally made maple syrup. Even if it isn't very nutritious, this substantial supper at the sugar shack is certainly worth trying.

7. Cretons

Cretons, a delightful cold pork spread, are often served with toast for breakfast. The forcemeat-style pork mixture, similar to French rillettes, also adds sliced onions and spices like cinnamon and cloves for added oomph.

Cretons are great on crackers, crostini bread, and toast. The spread, similar to pâte, is wonderful served on a shared charcuterie board, maybe with some mustard and sliced pickles. Other frequent names for the dish are Gorton, Corton, and Cretonnade.

8. Tarte au sucre (sugar pie)

Tarte au sucre is a delicious sugary pie popular in Quebec, particularly in Quebec City. With one notable variation, the traditional dish is similar to northern

France's tarte au sucre. Instead of utilizing regular sugar, the French-Canadian version uses maple syrup as its principal component.

The single crust of the pie is often laden with egg, flour, and large quantities of sticky maple syrup. Several patisseries lavishly add whipped cream to their baked items for a richer, fatter taste. This recipe, like many of the greatest Quebecois recipes, is not suitable for anyone attempting to lose weight.

9. **Tire sur la neige (maple taffy)**

Maple taffy, a combination of maple syrup and snow, is the most Quebecois thing possible. To commemorate the approach of spring, local restaurants put up little open-air taffy booths towards the end of winter. Furthermore, the meal is popular in sugar shacks, particularly in rural Quebec.

Chefs prepare this delectable seasonal dish by pouring boiling maple syrup over a new covering of snow. The cold shock quickly prevents the syrup from heating, causing it to thicken into a firm, chewy taffy. The youngsters will like this experience since it just takes a few seconds and is visually appealing.

10. **Pounding chômeur (poor man's pudding)**

Pouding chômeur is a traditional French-Canadian cake. Even though the name translates as "*poor man's pudding*," everyone, even the affluent, enjoys this delectable dish. The unusual term was developed during the Great Depression when its simple components were all most houses could afford.

Pouding chômeur is made with a white cake batter, cream sauce, and layers of maple syrup (rather than brown sugar). The mixture is spread over a pan and cooked in the oven until it puffs up into a big, fluffy cake. The classic dish may be found on the dessert menus of many Quebec City restaurants.

Best Restaurants in Quebec City

Some of the most well-known restaurants in the provincial capital are also among the top neighborhood restaurants in Quebec City. They're great venues to try the greatest Quebecois food the city has to offer, such as poutine, pâté chinois, and pounding chômeur.

You'll be in for a treat when you enjoy elegant French-Canadian food at these genuine neighborhood spots, all without breaking the bank. Meet the people, improve your accent, and eat your way across Quebec City by visiting these excellent eateries.

1. Le Bureau de Poste

Le Bureau de Poste in Quebec City dishes up top-notch pub fare in a quaint, ski lodge-style atmosphere. Tables constructed of tree trunks and wood panel walls create the appearance of being in a log cabin, and the energetic throng is drawn in by the inexpensive beverages. You shouldn't come here for a lovely, romantic supper since you can watch adolescent partygoers pounding shots off skis at the bar.

Despite being primarily a bar, Le Bureau de Poste is well-known for its superb food. The traditional pub meal from

Canada is available on the low-cost, flat-rate menu; for dessert, try the bacon poutine and a delicious parfait. Non-drinkers like the alcoholic-free, handmade iced tea.

Location: 296 Rue Saint-Joseph E, Québec, QC G1K 3A9, Canada

Open: *Daily from 11 am to 10 pm*

Phone: +1 418-914-6161

2. Les Trois Garçons

Les Trois Garçons' excellent gourmet burgers attract carnivorous trend-setters. Low lighting and exposed stone brick walls provide a cool, industrial-chic feel. It is designed in the manner of a New York/Paris restaurant. Because of the cheerful, enthusiastic service and a large range of specialty brews.

The massive Canadian-style burgers are the most popular menu item, which may be topped with everything from blue cheese to onion rings to maple-glazed bacon. Starving? The _Inter-travailleur burger_ is a monster. Less decadent options include poutine with cheddar curd or fish tartare.

Location: 1084 Rue Saint-Jean, Québec, QC G1R 1S4, Canada

Open: Monday–Thursday from 11.30 am to 9 pm, Friday–Saturday from 8 am to 10 pm, Sunday from 8 am to 9 pm

Phone: +1 418-692-3900

3. Poutineville

Poutineville is a well-known Canadian enterprise in Quebec City that offers the best, freshly sliced potatoes. In case you hadn't guessed, the eatery specializes in poutine, a robust meal of potato chips covered with cheese, meats, and sauce. While the company became well-known in Montreal, the Quebec City location has become a local favorite for comfort food.

Poutineville's allure stems from its unique approach. Instead of choosing a pre-made dish, you design your poutine recipe from a list of around 40 items. With excellent meats, premium Quebec cheese curds, and a range of potato and sauce choices, your creativity is allowed to run wild.

Location: 735 Rue Saint-Joseph E, Québec, QC G1K 3C6, Canada

Open: Sunday–Thursday from 11 am to 8 pm, Friday–Saturday from 11 am to 9.30 pm

Phone: +1 581-981-8188

4. L'Antiquaire Buffet

L'Antiquaire Buffet is well-known for its substantial home-style cuisine and inexpensive rates. The inconspicuous café is situated in the busy antique sector and is ideal for refueling after a vintage shopping expedition. Sit on the sidewalk terrace (only in the summer) and see how other customers move their goods.

The bulk of your favorite scrumptious Quebecois foods are available on the menu. One especially satisfying option is the _cipaille_, a classic deep-dish pie stuffed with high-quality meat or fowl. If you still have space for dessert, try the handmade crepes or sugar pie.

Location: 95 Rue Saint-Paul, Québec, QC G1K 3V8, Canada

Open: Sunday–Wednesday from 9 am to 4 pm, Thursday–Saturday from 6 am to 9 pm

Phone: +1 418-692-2661

5. Le Casse-Crêpe Breton

Le Casse-Crêpe Breton is your one-stop shop for real Quebecois crepes. In a pleasant ambiance, the small Old Town restaurant serves a buffet of scrumptious pancake-like delicacies. Because of the rapid service and reasonable costs, this is a nice pit stop for tourists visiting the city's historic core.

Customers may choose a flavor for breakfast, lunch, or dinner based on their mood. Among the delectable delicacies are fresh blueberries, strawberries, chocolate, and cream. Do you prefer something savory? Choose the crepe with Swiss cheese, mushrooms, and asparagus instead. Choose from an excellent range of beers on tap, regional wines, espresso coffee, and fresh juice to complement your meal.

Location: 1136 Rue Saint-Jean, Québec, QC G1R 1S4, Canada

Open: Monday–Friday from 7.30 am to 9.30 pm, Saturday–Sunday from 7 am to 9.30 pm

Phone: +1 418-692-0438

6. Phil Smoked Meat

Phil Smoked Meat delivers a broad menu of subs, sandwiches, pizza, pasta, and poutine, all created using the owner's famous smoked meats. The lovely, homely eatery pays tribute to classic diners with a comfortable tiled bar and cushy velvet chairs.

Phil's slow-smoked delights are enhanced by his handmade, acidic sauces. Although beef is the primary component in the bulk of meals, there are many vegetarian choices, particularly sandwiches. Do you want to reproduce the flavor at home? Place an order for a pound of smoked pork.

Location: 461 Rue Saint-Joseph E, Québec, QC G1K 3B6, Canada

Open: Tuesday and Wednesday from 11 am to 8.30 pm, Thursday–Saturday from 11 am to 9 pm (closed on Sundays and Mondays)

Phone: +1 418-523-4545

7. Bistro La Cohue

Bistro La Cohue in Quebec City serves excellent, reasonably priced Quebecois food. This modest bistro-style restaurant in a strip mall serves great food in a warm but plain setting.

The outstanding black pudding, flame-grilled shellfish, and slow-cooked bisque are among the menu's highlights. Save space for dessert at La Cohue, which offers a delectable crème brûlée. The sweet parfait is delicious. Bistro La Cohue's attractiveness is accentuated by courteous service and an excellent wine list.

Location: 3440 Chem. des Quatre-Bourgeois, Québec, QC G1W 4T3, Canada

Open: Monday–Friday from 11.30 am to 10 pm, Saturday–Sunday from 9.30 am to 10 pm

Phone: +1 418-659-1322

8. Bistro Hortus

Bistro Hortus delivers delectable farm-to-table food in a trendy yet relaxed atmosphere. The sleek, modern restaurant adheres to a rigorous eco-friendly concept, sourcing the bulk of its vegetables from the rooftop vegetable garden. The remaining components are supplied by local farmers. Workers even keep a rooftop bee-hive to fertilize crops and replenish decreasing populations.

The culinary staff prepares a well-balanced menu of classic French cuisine with a contemporary touch. There is a large assortment of vegetarian and vegan alternatives, and their roasted chicken meals are highly recommended. The stir-fried veggies with curd cheese, pearled barley, and black garlic sauce are a crowd-pleaser.

Location: 1190 Rue Saint-Jean, Québec, QC G1R 1S6, Canada

Open: Daily from 11 am to 11 pm

Phone: +1 418-692-5524

9. Beclub Bistro Bar

The charming Beclub Bistro Bar in Quebec City's Old Town is noted for its substantial meals. The stone and brick structure, which was erected in 1827, still has its original old-world splendor, making it an interesting spot to eat for visitors to the historic neighborhood.

Friendly service and a warm ambiance complement the home setting.

Every item on the menu was created in-house using seasonal veggies from local growers. The smoked meats are very good here, particularly the wild boar, a rare Quebecois delicacy. Allow the expert sommelier to pick the ideal wine from around 200 different varietals.

Location: 17 Rue Saint-Stanislas, Québec, QC G1R 4G7, Canada

Open: Tuesday–Saturday from 5 pm to 10 pm (closed on Sundays and Mondays)

Phone: +1 418-692-5488

10. Cuisine du Marché

Cuisine du Marché means "*market-fresh cuisine*" in English, and this stellar meat-loving venue doesn't disappoint. The owners source their uber-tender beef and produce straight from local farmers, ensuring each dish is truly fresh. If you can't make it to the reasonably priced restaurant (it's across the bridge in Levis), keep an eye out for the mobile food truck.

Pulled Wagyu beef is the house's specialty – each delectable morsel comes cooked to perfection. Other must-try carnivorous cuts include sirloin or flank steak. If red meat isn't your thing, you can try the scallops or lobster.

Location: 153 Rte Marie-Victorin, Saint-Nicolas, Quebec G7A 2T3, Canada

Open: *Thursday and Sunday from 5 pm to 6 pm, Friday–Saturday from 5 pm to 10 pm (closed Monday–Wednesday)*

Phone: +1 418-836-5959

Cafes and Bars

Quebec City is not just famous for its cuisine but also for its lively bar and cafe scene. The city offers a wide range of bars and cafes, from cozy local hangouts to trendy spots with a modern vibe. Whether you're looking for a spot to grab a quick coffee, relax with a drink, or dance the night away, Quebec City has plenty of options to choose from.

For coffee lovers, there are numerous cafes dotted around the city. Some of the best include **Brulerie Saint-Roch,** which offers a cozy atmosphere and freshly roasted coffee, and **Paillard,** which is known for its delicious pastries and sandwiches. If you're looking for a unique coffee experience, make sure to visit **La**

Finca, a coffee roaster that specializes in Latin American blends.

If you're in the mood for a drink, Quebec City's bar scene has plenty to offer. One of the most popular spots is **Le Cercle**, which serves up craft beers, cocktails, and live music in a relaxed and casual setting. For something more upscale, head to **Le Sam Bistro,** located in the iconic Fairmont Le Chateau Frontenac, for a cocktail with a view of the St. Lawrence River.

For those who love to dance, Quebec City has a variety of nightclubs and bars with a lively atmosphere. One of the most popular spots is **Le Dagobert,** which offers multiple dance floors, live DJs, and a wide selection of drinks. Another great option is **Le Drague Cabaret Club**.

Overall, Quebec City's bar and cafe scene offers something for everyone, from cozy and laidback to trendy and upbeat. With so many options to choose from, visitors are sure to find their perfect spot for a drink or a coffee in this vibrant city.

Chapter 4

Shopping in Quebec City

Shopping in Quebec City is an experience unlike any other. The city is home to a vibrant and eclectic mix of shops and boutiques, offering everything from high-end designer brands to locally made artisanal goods. With so many options to choose from, shopping in Quebec City is a must-do activity for visitors to the city.

One of the best places to start your shopping adventure in Quebec City is in the historic district of **Old Quebec**. This charming neighborhood is full of unique shops and boutiques, offering everything from handmade jewelry and clothing to locally produced food and drink. Some of the most popular shops in Old Quebec include **Simons,** a department store with a wide range of high-quality clothing and accessories, and **La Maison Simons**, a local boutique that specializes in handmade leather goods.

Another great shopping destination in Quebec City is **Quartier Petit Champlain**, a quaint and charming neighborhood filled with colorful buildings and cobblestone streets. This area is known for its local artisans and small boutiques, offering a wide range of unique and handmade products. Some of the most popular shops in Quartier Petit Champlain include **La Petite Cabane a Sucre de Quebec,** a store that specializes in maple syrup and maple products, and **Atelier Boutique Cuir Danier,** a leather goods shop that produces high-quality bags and accessories.

For those looking for luxury shopping, Quebec City has plenty of options as well. One of the best places to indulge in high-end shopping is at **Place Ste-Foy**, a large indoor shopping center that houses a variety of designer brands and luxury stores.

Finally, for those looking to experience Quebec City's local culture and heritage, the city has a variety of markets and artisanal shops to explore. **The Marche du Vieux-Port,** for example, is a farmers' market that sells fresh local produce, meats, and cheeses, as well as handmade crafts and souvenirs. **The rue du Tresor** is another popular destination for local arts

Quebec City Travel Guide 2023

and crafts, with a wide range of artists and artisans selling their work along this charming street.

In conclusion, shopping in Quebec City is a unique and unforgettable experience. From luxury brands to local artisans, the city has something for everyone. With so many options to choose from, visitors are sure to find the perfect souvenir or gift to take home with them.

Chapter 5

Day Trips and Excursions from Quebec City

Quebec City is undoubtedly one of the most beautiful and fascinating cities in North America, but there's much more to the province of Quebec than just its capital. From charming villages to natural wonders, there's no shortage of day trips and excursions to take from Quebec City. Here are some of the best:

1. Montmorency Falls

Located just a few minutes from Quebec City, Montmorency Falls is a breathtaking natural wonder that you can't miss. The falls are 83 meters high, which is taller than Niagara Falls, and there are several ways to experience them. Take a cable car to the top of the falls, walk across a suspension bridge, or climb the stairs to the base of the falls for a truly immersive experience.

2. Île d'Orléans

Île d'Orléans is a picturesque island located just a few kilometers east of Quebec City. The island is known for its stunning views, historic architecture, and agricultural heritage. Take a leisurely drive around the island and stop at local farms and artisanal shops to sample the island's famous maple products, ciders, and cheeses.

3. Charlevoix Region

Located just over an hour's drive northeast of Quebec City, the Charlevoix region is a paradise for nature lovers. This stunning area is home to rolling hills, scenic coastal roads, and several national parks. Take a whale-watching tour, hike through the mountains, or visit one of the region's charming villages for a taste of rural Quebec life.

4. Sainte-Anne-de-Beaupré Shrine

Located just 30 minutes east of Quebec City, the Sainte-Anne-de-Beaupré Shrine is one of the most important pilgrimage sites in North America. The shrine is dedicated to Saint Anne, the patron saint of Quebec, and draws thousands of visitors each year. Explore the beautiful basilica and chapel, visit the museum, or light a candle and say a prayer.

5. Tadoussac

Located about 3 hours northeast of Quebec City, Tadoussac is a charming village located at the confluence of the St. Lawrence and Saguenay rivers. This historic village is known for its stunning scenery, whale-watching tours, and charming streets. Visit the Tadoussac Marine Mammal Interpretation Centre to learn more about the region's marine life, or take a kayak tour to explore the rugged coastline.

6. Parc National de la Jacques-Cartier

Located just 30 minutes north of Quebec City, the Parc National de la Jacques-Cartier is a stunning wilderness area that's perfect for outdoor enthusiasts. The park is home to over 100 km of hiking trails, ranging from easy walks to challenging backcountry hikes. Explore the park's breathtaking valleys and mountains, or go fishing, canoeing, or camping.

7. Wendake

Wendake is a First Nations reserve located just outside of Quebec City. The reserve is home to the Huron-Wendat people, who have lived in the area for centuries. Visitors can learn about the Huron-Wendat culture at the Huron-Wendat Museum. There are also several restaurants and shops located on the reserve.

8. Saint-Ferréol-les-Neiges

Located just 45 minutes north of Quebec City, Saint-Ferréol-les-Neiges is a charming village located at the base of Mont-Sainte-Anne. This area is known for its skiing, snowboarding, and other winter sports, but there's plenty to do here in the summer months as well. Visit the village's charming shops and restaurants, hike through the surrounding mountains, or take a scenic gondola ride to the top of the ski resort for stunning views of the region.

9. Village Vacances Valcartier

Village Vacances Valcartier is a water park located about an hour's drive from Quebec City. The park offers a variety of water slides, pools, and activities for all ages. There is also a campground, hotel, and restaurants located at the park.

These are just a few of the many day trips and excursions you can take from Quebec City. Whether you're interested in nature, history, or culture, there's something for everyone just a short drive from this beautiful city.

Fun Things to Do in Quebec City

Quebec City, the capital of French Canada, has a long history of being a hub for artists, chefs, crafters, and microbrewers. Did you know it's also the only fortified city north of Mexico and home to the world's most renowned hotel? There's no other place like this in North America!

Visit the stately Chateau Frontenac, pick up a memento at a local gallery, or see a show at one of the city's ancient theater clubs for a sense of Quebec City's uniqueness. This is a location where European and American cultures coexist. Get your first taste of the delectable poutine while eating on a boat down the Saint Lawrence River.

Since it was established by a French adventurer in 1608, you can't help but notice the effect it has had on this city, from the building to the dialect to the cuisine to the culture! To put it plainly, it is enticing.

Check out the whole list since there are so many interesting things to do in Quebec City, whether you want to walk around the picturesque Old Town and historic Île d'Orléans or marvel at the Montmorency Falls!

1. **Travel back in time by seeing Old Quebec City**

As one of your initial acts, you should go to Old Quebec City, Canada's only entirely fortified town. This location has historically noteworthy architecture.

Don't miss the Plains of Abraham, Parliament Hill, and the boutiques on Rue de Petit-Champlain, where you may ride the Old Quebec Funicular cable car.

The historic town is a UNESCO World Heritage site because it was the beginning point of French North American culture over 400 years ago. There are several important monuments and well-known places, and it is separated into Upper and Lower Town sections.

2. See the massive fortifications that surround the city
Old Quebec City is Canada's only walled city, and seeing the 400-year-old walls up close is amazing.

The Upper Town's 4.6 km of fortifications include beautiful gates carved into them.

The original four are still present, and more have been added throughout time.

Don't miss out on the chance to photograph these amazing walls!

3. View the exquisite collection of religious art in the Basilique-Cathedrale Notre-Dame-de-Quebec

The majestic Basilique-Cathedrale Notre-Dame-De-Quebec serves as the primary cathedral for the Quebec Roman Catholic Archdiocese and has undergone various repairs throughout the years. There are some wonderful religious pieces of art there.

All of the bishops of the Diocese of Quebec, as well as several other notable personalities, are buried here.

The church was completed in 1647, although it has undergone repairs as a consequence of wars, bombings, and fires since then. The neoclassical architecture, beautiful glass windows, and stunning angel statues of the Catholic Church are now something to see.

4. Walk over the waterfalls at Parc de la Chute-Montmorency

Parc de la Chute-Montmorency, often known as Montmorency Falls Park, is a must-see attraction in Quebec. The whole promenade may be walked over the beautiful falls, which are significantly higher than Niagara Falls, Canada's other well-known waterfall.

If you're not afraid of heights, ride the cable car and check out the zip line while you're there.

5. Climb to the highest point in the whole city at Observatoire de la Capitale

The Capital Observatory in Quebec City is the city's highest point. From here, you can see the Laurentians, the Saint Lawrence River, the Island of Orleans, and the Appalachian Foothills, as well as Parliament Hill and the rest of the city.

They also provide a selection of on-site activities that will educate you about Quebec's history and culture.

6. Visit the massive and well-known Château Frontenac Hotel

The Fairmont Chateau Frontenac, one of Canada's most well-known hotels, is often rated among the hotels with the most images shot throughout the world.

For almost a century, the Chateau Frontenac has served as a house for people from all over the globe, and its interesting history is on display for travelers to enjoy. It is without a doubt one of the top things to do in Quebec City.

Although guided excursions are always available, who wouldn't want to stay at the same hotel as celebrities like Charlie Chaplin and Sir Paul McCartney?

7. **Visit the Gorgeous Basilica in Sainte-Anne-de-Beaupré**

Sainte-Anne-de-Beaupre, a little town near Quebec City, has numerous interesting attractions, including the Sainte-Anne-de-Beaupre Basilica and Shrine.

The Basilica's Scala Santa, the steps that Jesus climbed to Pilate's praetorium, and the hundreds of votive lights that burn day and night in recollection are just a few of the reasons to come.

Remember to pay a visit to the memorial chapel, where centuries ago French pilgrims rested!

8. **Visit the Quebec National Assembly at the Parliament Building**

If you've ever wanted to see where the laws of Quebec are discussed, go visit the Quebec National Assembly in the Parliament Building.

The words "*je me souviens,*" which translates to "*I remember*," were etched above the main entrance more than a century ago. This is Quebec's campaign slogan.

There are public tours of the institution and its surroundings, as well as a constant program of events.

9. Take to the Saint Lawrence River on a boat tour

The Saint Lawrence River in Canada is breathtaking. Numerous boat cruises depart from Quebec City's Old Port and take you down the river to some of the city's most well-known attractions, including Chateau Frontenac and the stunning Montmorency Falls.

A typical tour lasts around an hour and includes live commentary from a qualified local guide.

This massive body of water is separated into three sections over its 1,197 km length. The river passes through Quebec City before draining into the St. Lawrence

Estuary and the Atlantic Ocean, both of which are located between Quebec and Anticosti Islan.

10. **Visit the Plains of Abraham at Battlefields Park**

Visit the epic Plains of Abraham Battle on September 13, 1759, as well as numerous other key English-French conflicts.

Discover why the path of the Seven Years' War was substantially changed in this region. They do historically realistic reenactments using toy weapons and costume.

11. **Check out the indigenous art collection at the MNBAQ**

The Musée National des Beaux-Arts du Québec is honored to serve as the living memory of Quebec's art and its artists.

Its collection has almost 42,000 different pieces, including an amazing collection of Inuit artwork. Check their activities calendar before you attend since their exhibitions are always changing.

The museum is organized into four sections: the <u>Central Pavilion,</u> the <u>Gérard Morisset Pavilion</u>, the <u>Charles Baillairgé Pavilion,</u> and the <u>Pierre Lassonde Pavilion</u> (which houses the Librairie-Boutique and stores offering art, crafts, and books on the topic.

12. Explore the charming villages that makeup Île d'Orléan

Ile d'Orleans is remarkable since it was one of the first locations in Quebec to be colonized by French people. Six small settlements are linked to one another by a 67-kilometer circle.

The island is home to four vineyards, a 300-year-old mansion, the remains of a shipyard where hundreds of rowboats were once manufactured, and many more sight.

Choose from incredible activities to and around Ile d'Orleans, such as culinary experiences, wine tastings, and cycling excursions, or do it alone (the drive from the city takes around 30 minutes.

13. Discover the greatest coffee shops for recharging your battery

If you're a coffee lover or connoisseurs seeking the greatest coffee-replenishing spots in town, go no further.

Enjoy a delicious cup of coffee from Nektar, whether you like drip or fudge brew, or purchase a bag of their locally roasted beans. Maelstrm café, a specialty coffee shop with a cocktail bar if you're feeling cheerful, was inspired by the simple Nordic style.

Cafe Saint-Henri, a professional roaster, and micro-roastery, promotes feelings of tranquillity in addition to dishing up some pretty great coffee. On-site coffee training is available.

Café Pekoe boasts a broad cuisine that pays homage to numerous Asian locations, whether you're seeking a Vietnamese banh mi sandwich or renowned bubble tea.

14. Take a hop-on, hop-off bus to go from one tourist attraction to another

Quebec City, one of Canada's oldest cities, is home to numerous notable historical sites. Fortunately, the city offers a variety of flexible bus routes as well as several terminals where tourists may board and exit.

After you get in Place Royale from the walled section of Old Quebec, you will have plenty of time to sightsee.

The double-decker bus stops at 14 locations, enabling you to alight and see up to 30 attractions, including Notre-Dame-des-Victoires Church, Palais Montcalm, Martello Towers, Fontaine de la Place d'Armes, Quartier Petit Champlain, and many more.

15. **See the birthplace of French Canada, Place Royale**

Place Royale is one of Canada's oldest and most well-known landmarks. This well-known public plaza, often known as the "Birthplace of French America," exemplifies both Quebec's unique and convoluted past as well as the province's relevance to Canada.

The fact that so much of the old structure can still be visible demonstrates how both British and French colonists had an effect throughout time.

Take lots of photos as you walk the cobblestone walkways of the ancient Market Square, which was originally named Place du Marché when it was built in 1608. The majestic Notre-Dame-des-Victoires Church, erected in stone in 1688, is also close.

16. Take a walk at Terrasse Dufferin

The charming Terrasse Dufferin, located between the Saint Lawrence River and Chateau Frontenac, has a lengthy history.

In the summer and winter, both tourists and residents visit this attractive site. There is much to see and do, including a medieval crypt under the Terrasse. In the winter, there are wooden sledding slopes for tobogganing.

17. Spend the day shopping in Quartier Petit-Champlain

If you want to go shopping, you should head to Quartier Petit-Champlain.

This area's small alleyways and century-old residences are lined with lovely stores that beg to be explored.

The Quartier Petit-Champlain is attractively lighted all year, but it particularly sparkles during the Christmas season.

18. Go whale watching in the springtime

Every spring, hundreds of whales migrate to the Quebec coast, especially Charlevoix, to play and eat krill.

Numerous whale-watching trips depart from Quebec City's Old Port, bringing you up close and personal with over six distinct species, including the spectacular blue whale.

Make sure to check availability and book early for these tours since they sell out rapidly!

19. Take a quick ferry journey to Quebec City

There is no better view of Old Quebec from the Saint Lawrence River than what you receive on the dirt-cheap, 12-minute Quebec City Ferry excursion.

You'll just have enough time to whip out your camera and photograph prominent landmarks.

The boat operates all year, but viewing Old Quebec lighted up from the lake is particularly beautiful around the holidays.

20. **Go for the full thermal experience at a spa**

Quebec City, like other big towns, has a wide range of wonderful spa alternatives for both visitors and residents.

You won't want to miss the calm thermal experience provided by Old Quebec's _Strom Nordic Spa_, one of the city's most popular spas and conveniently situated directly on the Saint Lawrence River.

Because of Quebec's unique temperature and surroundings, several spas in and around this northern city have a winter theme. As a consequence, many package deals include winter activities such as ice canoeing or snowmobiling.

21. **Get your hands wet in the aquarium**

The underwater paradise of the Quebec Aquarium will appeal to both youngsters and adults. They have a diverse range of animals. Some species, such as starfish and horseshoe crabs, may be touched, while polar bears should not be approached too closely!

They also provide a variety of instructional activities, as well as games and obstacle courses in the water.

22. **Kayak along one of Quebec's beautiful rivers or lakes**

The province of Quebec is practically totally covered with beautiful lakes, rivers, and woods. Although the majority of it is protected territory, there are various locations where you may rent or purchase a kayak and go out into the open sea.

You may also kayak along the Saint Lawrence River and enjoy the lovely views of Old Quebec City and its fortifications.

A common alternative for kayaking vacations is to fly to Orleans Island. If you pick a trip with a tour guide, your three-hour water adventure includes a double-sea kayak, paddle, life jacket, and even a waterproof backpack.

23. **Go to a Videotron Center hockey game or concert**

The Videotron Centre is one of the city's more recent marvels, and the arena is one of the greatest venues to attend a live concert or hockey game! Many of the older structures, on the other hand, are decades old and dripping with history and time.

Its glass entry halls, which allow in plenty of natural light, are a standout feature.

Because it is the home of the Quebec Remparts ice hockey club, you may sometimes watch a live game being played here. In addition to athletic sports, the vast stadium has been adapted to hold musical events and concerts.

24. **Have an exhilarating round of Laser Tag**

Laser Game Evolution is ready to demonstrate that playing Laser Tag is more than just a goofy kid's game after more than 25 years in business.

The game is built with cutting-edge, lightweight technology to promote comfort and precision, and its animation team is dedicated to making every experience enjoyable for all players. They have several sites around Quebec.

25. **Spend the whole day at Mega Parc having fun**

Méga Parc, Quebec City's biggest indoor amusement park, features rides and entertainment for guests of all ages.

An arcade, a roller coaster, a Ferris wheel, and an ice skating rink are among the entertaining family activities offered. There's also laser tag and bumper cars!

If you're seeking true heart-pounding thrills or family-friendly activities in Quebec, this amusement park will not disappoint.

Chapter 6

Practical Information

If you're planning a trip to Quebec City, there are a few practical pieces of information that may be helpful for you to know beforehand. Here are some tips to help you prepare for your visit:

1. Currency: The official currency in Quebec is the Canadian Dollar (CAD). You can exchange currency at banks, exchange offices, and many hotels. Most businesses accept major credit cards as well.

2. Language: The official language in Quebec is French, although many people also speak English. It's a good idea to learn a few basic French phrases before your trip, as it can be helpful when communicating with locals.

3. Time Zone: Quebec City is located in the Eastern Time Zone, which is four hours behind Coordinated Universal Time (UTC-4).

4. Climate: Quebec City experiences four distinct seasons, with warm summers and cold winters. The best time to visit is typically from May to October, when the weather is milder and more pleasant.

5. Transportation: Quebec City has a public transportation system that includes buses and trains. Taxis and ride-sharing services like Uber are also available. If you plan to explore the city on foot, be sure to wear comfortable shoes as many of the streets are cobblestone.

6. Safety: Quebec City is generally a safe destination for tourists, but it's always a good idea to be aware of your surroundings and take precautions to protect your belongings. Avoid leaving valuables in plain sight in your car, and keep an eye on your belongings in crowded areas.

7. Health: Quebec City has a good healthcare system, but it's always a good idea to travel with travel insurance. If you require medical attention while in Quebec, there are several hospitals and clinics available.

8. Electricity: Quebec City uses the same electrical outlets as the rest of Canada and the United States, with a voltage of 120V and a frequency of 60Hz. If you're traveling from another country, you may need to bring an adapter for your electronics.

9. **Wi-Fi:** Most hotels, restaurants, and cafes in Quebec City offer free Wi-Fi, so you can stay connected during your visit.

10. **Customs**: Quebec City has its own unique customs and traditions, so it's a good idea to learn about them before your trip. For example, it's customary to greet people with a kiss on each cheek, and tipping is generally expected in restaurants and for taxi rides.

By keeping these practical tips in mind, you'll be well-prepared for your visit to Quebec City and able to make the most of your time there. Enjoy your trip!

Chapter 7

Basic Phrases for Visitors in Quebec

As a visitor to Quebec, it's helpful to know some basic French phrases to help you navigate the city and communicate with locals. While many Quebecois are bi-lingual and speak English as well, using some French phrases can show your appreciation for the local culture and make your interactions with locals more pleasant. Here are some basic phrases for visitors in Quebec:

1. Bonjour - Hello
This is a polite greeting that you can use throughout the day. It's pronounced "bohn-zhoor."

2. **Comment ça va?** - How are you?
This is a common question you can ask when you meet someone. It's pronounced "ko-mahn sah vah."

3. **Merci** - Thank you
This is a polite way to express gratitude. It's pronounced "mehr-see."

4. **S'il vous plaît** - Please
This is a polite way to make a request. It's pronounced "seel voo pleh."

5. **Excusez-moi** - Excuse me
This is a polite way to get someone's attention or to apologize. It's pronounced "ex-koo-zay mwah."

6. **Parlez-vous anglais?** - Do you speak English?

This is a helpful question to ask if you're having trouble communicating in French. It's pronounced "par-lay voo ahn-glay."

7. Je ne parle pas français - I don't speak French

If you're not comfortable speaking French, you can use this phrase to explain that you don't speak the language. It's pronounced "juh nuh parl pah frahn-say."

8. Où est...? - Where is...?

This is a useful question to ask when you're looking for a specific location. For example, "Où est la gare?" means "Where is the train station?" It's pronounced "oo eh...?"

9. Combien ça coûte? - How much does it cost?

Quebec City Travel Guide 2023

This is a useful question to ask when you're shopping or ordering food. It's pronounced "kohm-bee-ahn sah koot?"

10. Au revoir - Goodbye
This is a polite way to say goodbye to someone. It's pronounced "oh ruh-vwah."

Other Useful Phrases

- **Yes** - Oui (wee)

- **No** - Non (nohn)

- **I'm sorry** - Je suis désolé(e) (zhuh swee day-zoh-lay)

- **Do you speak English?** - Parlez-vous anglais? (par-lay voo ahn-glay?)

- **I don't understand** - Je ne comprends pas (zhuh nuh kohn-prahn pah)

- **How much does this cost?** - Combien ça coûte? (kohm-bee-ehn sah koot?)

- **Where is the restroom?** - Où sont les toilettes? (oo sohn lay twa-let?)

- **Can you help me?** - Pouvez-vous m'aider? (poo-vay voo may-day?)

- **I would like...** - Je voudrais... (zhuh voo-dray...)

- **The bill, please** - L'addition, s'il vous plaît (lah-dee-see-yohn, seel voo play)

- **Cheers!** - Santé! (sahn-tay)

- **Bon appétit!** - Bon appétit! (bon ah-peh-tee)

- **Have a good day** - Bonne journée (bun zhur-nay)

- **See you later** - À plus tard (ah ploo tar)

Remember, the people of Quebec City appreciate it when visitors make an effort to speak their language. Even if you only learn a few basic phrases, it can make a big difference in how you are perceived and can enhance your overall experience in the city.

Conclusion

As your journey through Quebec City comes to an end, it is impossible not to feel the longing for more. This city has a way of capturing your heart with its charm, history, and natural beauty. From the cobblestone streets to the towering Château Frontenac, Quebec City is a place that will stay with you long after you leave.

You have explored the city's rich history, sampled its delicious cuisine, and wandered through its picturesque parks. You have taken in the beauty of the St. Lawrence River, marveled at the architecture of the city's historic buildings, and experienced the warmth of Quebecois hospitality.

Quebec City Travel Guide 2023

As you depart, take with you the memories of your time in Quebec City. Remember the sound of the French language, the aroma of freshly baked bread and pastries, and the feel of the cool breeze on your face as you stood at the edge of the river. These memories will keep you connected to this beautiful city and its people.

Whether you come back to Quebec City to experience the magic of the winter carnival, enjoy the colors of fall, or explore the city during the long summer days, you will always be welcomed with open arms. So, until we meet again, au revoir and merci, Quebec City.

Quebec City Travel Guide 2023

Made in the USA
Coppell, TX
22 May 2023